Safe Return
HOME

Other Crankshaft Books

I've Still Got It!

. . . And One Slice with Anchovies!

Crankshaft

Safe Return
HOME

An Inspirational Book for Caregivers
of Alzheimer's

by Tom Batiuk and Chuck Ayers

Andrews McMeel
Publishing

Kansas City

www.andrewsmcmeel.com

98 99 00 01 02 RDC 10 9 8 7 6 5 4 3 2 1

Library of Congress Cataloging-in-Publication Data

Batiuk, Tom.
    Safe return home : an inspirational book for caregivers of Alzheimer's / by Tom Batiuk and Chuck Ayers.
        p.   cm.
    ISBN 0-8362-6913-6 (hd)
        1. Alzheimer's disease—Patients—Care—Comic books, strips, etc.   2. Alzheimer's disease—Patients—Humor.   3. Batiuk, Tom. Crankshaft.   Selections.   I. Ayers, Chuck (Charles W.)   II. Title.
RC523.2.B38   1998
362.1'96831—DC21   98-3785
                                                                                 CIP

ATTENTION: SCHOOLS AND BUSINESSES

Andrews McMeel books are available at quantity discounts with bulk purchase for educational, business, or sales promotional use. For information, please write to: Special Sales Department, Andrews McMeel Publishing, 4520 Main Street, Kansas City, Missouri 64111.

*For those who live with a shadow
across their mind.*

❧

*F*oreword

Other than my own, there are few comic strips around I wish *I* were doing. One of them is the elegant *Crankshaft* which, by coincidence, is the subject of this inelegant foreword.

I wish I could write like Tom Batiuk!

I wish I could draw like Chuck Ayers!

I wish my talent and perspicacity were such that I could convey serious, painful, often soul-trying family situations in terms so stylish and gentle as to make them acceptable even on the comics page, long regarded as the kindergarten of the newspaper.

Not so long ago, daring to explore such subjects would have been grounds for a comic strip practitioner's dismissal from the public prints. In fact, even today, cartoonists with lesser sensibilities than these two men would be accused of trivialization.

But Batiuk and Ayers are the Lewis and Clark of our business, good enough and fearless enough to take their readers onto some very dark waters . . . illiteracy . . . familial ingratitude and disappointment . . . plain, garden-variety crankiness. And, in these very pages, the most heartbreaking of all: the impact of Alzheimer's disease.

Now, having said all that, I can still promise that you're going to laugh a lot while reading this extraordinary book. But yes, yes, you will cry. Starting on page twelve.

—*Mell Lazarus,* president of the National Cartoonists Society
and creator of *Momma* and *Miss Peach*

Ed Crankshaft takes his friend Ralph and his neighbor Lillian to visit Ralph's wife, Helen, and Lillian's sister, Lucy, at the nursing home.

11

12

Your *Crankshaft* is wonderful—so original and true to life. . . . Your recent strip with the Barrie quote: "God gave us memory that we might have roses in December" carried the most meaning and emotion of any comic I've ever seen. . . . Those three little frames speak volumes. And Crankshaft did not have to say a word—his hand on his friend's shoulder says it all. There is a lesson there for us all. It is surely cartooning at its best and highest level. . . .

Many thanks for your special cartoon.

—*Anonymous*

HELEN PROBABLY WON'T REMEMBER THAT TODAY IS OUR ANNIVERSARY.

WE'RE STILL MARRIED, BUT AS HER ALZHEIMER'S GETS WORSE....

I REALLY DON'T HAVE HER ANYMORE.

HAPPY ANNIVERSARY, HELEN....

I HOPE YOU LIKE IT....

IT'S ONE OF THOSE SLINKY FREDERICK'S OF HOLLYWOOD FLANNEL NIGHTIES!

ACTUALLY, I WAS GOING TO GET YOU A MERCEDES FOR OUR ANNIVERSARY... BUT THEY WON'T LET YOU HAVE CARS HERE.

SIGH YOU NEVER COULD TAKE A JOKE...

I TOOK YOU....

16

I want to thank you for a recent *Crankshaft* that appeared in our Minneapolis paper, the *Star Tribune*. It showed a side of *Crankshaft* that I've not seen, perhaps because I am a caregiver of a victim of Alzheimer's and I do not always finish the day's paper.

One of the ways I have learned to cope with my husband's illness is to recall all the good memories—"roses in December" are in my mental vase. . . .

I have concluded that one or both of you have a loved one suffering from this disease. There is so much compassion here—that Crankshaft accompanies his pal to "Sunny Days" shows his humanity—and in the last panel there old Crank was with his arm on his friend's shoulder. I weep as I write this just as I did when I first saw your cartoon.

My thanks and my admiration.

—*Mary Ellen Jette*

Comic strips are not always meant to be humorous but often are created to provide insight into the human condition.

And that is what Batiuk and Ayers have done with this series of strips. They gave us a caring, poignant look at the effects of Alzheimer's disease on the person with the disease and on the family and close friends. The final strip on this subject, with the observation that "God gave us a memory so that we could have roses in the winter," was an ironic statement, not black humor.

So many of us live with the dread of Alzheimer's, either for ourselves or for our loved ones. Batiuk and Ayers spoke to us, recognizing our fears and helping us to understand them.

Batiuk and Ayers brought compassion and enlightenment to us before with the series on illiteracy. Obviously, they are astute students of people and use the comic strip format to reflect on our humanity and to help us understand our individual realities and the realities of others.

Thank goodness they do. May they continue to do so.

—*Phyllis Thornley*, Minneapolis, Minnesota

*A*ny two people who have the sensitivity and compassion to turn their cartooning talents into a poignant but humorous look at Alzheimer's disease makes me feel they are real friends.

We passed your cartoons around our Alzheimer's group, and for the ones who hadn't seen it, it touched them deeply, yet made them laugh.

As you might have gathered, I have someone with Alzheimer's in my family. My dear husband of forty-three years is in what they call the "final stages," whatever that means, as people with this terrible disease can go on for twenty years.

I had him at home for ten of those years, and, believe me, we had fun along with the pain, as I too, have a sense of humor, especially about life, and know that you can't take it all too seriously.

We had many good years together, and when he first started some of the most terrible symptoms, I had to tell myself that repeatedly, because otherwise a sense of frustration and depression can set in.

I am sure one of you fellows, or maybe both, have had someone who has this disease close to you, or you couldn't have done these cartoons, which are right on target every time.

Now, don't think I haven't been an admirer of your strip *before* these cartoons were pictured, because I have always *loved* old Crankshaft and his cranky ways.

And, not only can people in my age group identify with him, but people of all ages; my kids are real fans, too.

So, keep up the good work, know you are appreciated and especially by the many, many caretakers of Alzheimer's patients. . . . I hope they are writing in to tell of their appreciation, too. If they aren't, well it's only because they are too darned busy taking care of a loved one.

—*Ruth Harris,* San Clemente, California

THIS IS THE MOST ENJOYABLE PART OF THE DAY FOR ME!

THERE'S NOTHING MORE RELAXING THAN A GOOD BOOK...A WARM CUP OF TEA...

AND, OF COURSE THE RUMBALL DOESN'T HURT EITHER!

BATIUK & AYERS

YOU KNOW, LIL...SEEING THAT SNOW COME DOWN OUT THERE REMINDS ME OF WHEN WE USED TO GO SLEDDING OVER AT BUZZARD'S GORGE!

I WAS ALWAYS SO PROUD OF YOU!

BATIUK & AYERS

YOU WERE THE ONLY GIRL WHO WAS BRAVE ENOUGH TO SLED WITH THE BOYS DOWN NOBOTTOM HILL!

OH, GO ON...

SLEDDING AT BUZZARD'S GORGE WAS ALWAYS A LOT OF FUN....

BUT I'M AFRAID THAT OUR SLEDDING DAYS ARE A THING OF THE PAST!

BATIUK & AYERS

'OLD LIGHTNING' STILL SEEMS TO BE PRETTY SOLID!

IT LOOKS A LITTLE RUSTY AND CREAKY TO ME!

SQUEAK!

WELL, SO ARE WE!

IT LOOKS LIKE THE McKENZIE SISTERS ARE GOING TO THE GROCERY STORE WITH A SLED TO BRING BACK THEIR GROCERIES!

'THAT'S REALLY SENSIBLE OF THEM NOT TO TAKE UNNECESSARY RISKS BY GOING OUT IN THEIR CAR ON A DAY LIKE THIS!'

OOOF!

WHUMP!

THAT WAS FUN... LET'S DO IT AGAIN!

OKAY... BUT THIS TIME I GET TO BE ON TOP!

27

WHEN YOU GO BACK TO A PLACE FROM YOUR CHILDHOOD IT USUALLY SEEMS SMALLER THAN YOU REMEMBER IT...

EXCEPT FOR NOBOTTOM HILL!

I'LL BET OLD LIGHTNING COULD STILL DO IT!

LIL'! NO!!

LILLIAN! NO!! YOU CAN'T GO DOWN NOBOTTOM HILL!

SURE I CAN! I'VE JUST GOT TO REMEMBER TO SHIFT MY WEIGHT AND NOT LOOK OUT OVER THE GORGE WHEN I MAKE THE TURN!

NO! YOU'VE GOT TO REMEMBER THAT WAS OVER FIFTY YEARS AGO!

LIL'... PLEASE DON'T DO THIS!!

YOU JUST GO AHEAD AND WALK BACK DOWN!

I'LL BE WAITING FOR YOU AT THE BOTTOM!

29

YOUR PLAYING SOUNDED ESPECIALLY NICE TODAY, LILLIAN!

THANK YOU... BUT I WAS REALLY HAVING A DIFFICULT TIME BECAUSE SOME OF THE STOPS WEREN'T WORKING!

THAT PROBABLY EXPLAINS WHY THE HYMNS SEEMED TO DRAG ON FOREVER!

33

TELL ME MORE ABOUT EUGENE, LUCY!

WELL... THE FIRST TIME I SAW EUGENE WAS ON A SUMMER EVENING IN JULY... HE WAS A FRIEND OF LILLY'S AND THEY INVITED ME TO GO DANCING WITH THEM AT THE WISTERIA BALLROOM AT SUMMIT BEACH PARK!

BATIUK & AYERS

I THOUGHT HE WAS THE MOST HANDSOMEST BOY I'D EVER SEEN!

WHEN WE ARRIVED AT THE WISTERIA BALLROOM, WE DISCOVERED THAT THEY WERE HAVING A DANCE CONTEST!

DANCE CONTEST TO-NITE

BATIUK & AYERS

EUGENE WANTED TO ENTER IT, BUT LILLY DIDN'T WANT TO!

ACTUALLY, LILLY WASN'T A VERY GOOD WALTZER BECAUSE SHE ALWAYS LIKED TO LEAD!

SINCE LILLY DIDN'T WANT TO ENTER THE DANCE CONTEST EUGENE ASKED ME!

Harold Nelson Aircrafters

WHAT DO YOU SAY, LUCY? SHALL WE GIVE IT A GO?

BATIUK & AYERS

SINCE EUGENE AND LILLY WERE JUST FRIENDS, I KNEW SHE WOULDN'T MIND IF I SAID I WOULD!

Harold Nelson Aircrafters

CRANKSHAFT ® BY BATIUK & AYERS

SO YOU AND EUGENE DECIDED TO ENTER THE DANCE CONTEST AT THE WISTERIA BALLROOM?

THAT'S RIGHT!

HOW ROMANTIC!

'HUNDREDS OF OTHER COUPLES SIGNED UP FOR THE DANCE CONTEST THAT NIGHT AT THE WISTERIA BALLROOM... BUT THE ONLY PERSON I COULD SEE WAS EUGENE!'

'I'LL NEVER FORGET HOW DAPPER AND HANDSOME HE LOOKED THAT NIGHT!'

THAT'S WHAT MY GRANDPA SAYS WHEN HE TALKS ABOUT THE FIRST TIME HE SAW MY GRANDMA!

HE SAY'S HE WAS MEMORIZED BY HER BEAUTY!

BATIUK & AYERS

36

NOW WHERE IS THAT HOT CHOCOLATE MIX? I CAN'T SEEM TO REMEMBER WHERE I PUT ANYTHING THESE DAYS!

SO WHAT HAPPENED AT THE DANCE CONTEST?

WHAT DANCE CONTEST?

THE ONE THAT YOU AND EUGENE ENTERED AT THE WISTERIA BALLROOM!

OH.... THAT DANCE CONTEST!

HUNDREDS OF COUPLES ENTERED THE DANCE CONTEST AT THE WISTERIA BALLROOM THAT NIGHT!

LILLY COULDN'T HAVE BEEN MORE THRILLED WHEN EUGENE AND I SURVIVED THE FIRST ROUND!

EACH DAY I'D HURRY HOME FROM MY JOB AT THE LAUNDRY AND EUGENE AND I WOULD PRACTICE FOR THAT EVENING'S CONTEST...

THEN THAT NIGHT WE'D COMPETE AT THE WISTERIA BALLROOM WITH THE OTHER DANCERS!

SOMETIMES, DURING BREAKS IN THE COMPETITION, WE'D GET A SCHOONER OF BEER AND GO OFF TO SIT AND WATCH THE MOONLIGHT ON THE LAKE!

37

FINALLY AFTER A WEEK OF GOING BACK AND COMPETING EVERY NIGHT, THE DANCE CONTEST WAS DOWN TO THE TEN BEST COUPLES!

EUGENE AND I KNEW THAT IF WE WANTED TO WIN WE WERE GOING TO HAVE TO USE OUR SECRET WEAPON!

SECRET WEAPON?

THE JITTERBUG!

THAT NIGHT, AT THE FINALS OF THE DANCE CONTEST, EUGENE AND I DID OUR JITTERBUG!

UNFORTUNATELY, THE OPERATORS OF THE BALLROOM THOUGHT THE JITTERBUG WAS AN INDECENT DANCE AND WE WERE REMOVED FROM THE COMPETITION! LILLY WAS CRUSHED AS WERE WE!

DID YOU AND EUGENE KEEP SEEING EACH OTHER AFTER THE DANCE CONTEST, LUCY?

OH, MY... LOOK AT HOW LATE IT'S GOTTEN! I'M AFRAID THAT'S ALL THE TIME WE HAVE FOR STITCHING TODAY?!

BYE...I'LL SEE YOU TOMORROW...

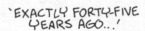

42

YOU THREW OUT **GRANDMOTHER'S LAMPSHADE!!?**

WELL...THERE WAS THIS ONE BIG BOX.... BUT DON'T WORRY! THE TRASH HASN'T BEEN PICKED UP YET!

I'LL JUST GO DOWN AND GET IT!

Grandma's Lampshade

IT'S GONE!!

THAT WAS A GENUINE **TIFFANY** LAMPSHADE! DO YOU HAVE ANY IDEA WHAT THAT WAS **WORTH**!?

HOW COULD YOU BE SO **STUPID**!!?

I'M NOT STUPID... I JUST GET CONFUSED AND FORGET THINGS!

DID YOU SEE THE McKENZIE SISTERS OUT THERE ARGUING ON THE TREELAWN?

YES.... I THINK THE WHOLE NEIGHBORHOOD WAS WATCHING!

THAT'S A SWITCH... USUALLY IT'S THE OTHER WAY AROUND!

43

CRANKSHAFT by BATIUK & AYERS

I'M SORRY ABOUT GIVING GRANDMOTHER'S LAMPSHADE AWAY, LIL!

I JUST DON'T SEEM TO BE THINKING RIGHT LATELY!

I DIDN'T REALIZE THAT GRANDMOTHER'S LAMPSHADE WAS SO VALUABLE....

BUT WHAT DID IT MATTER ALL HIDDEN AWAY IN A DARK ATTIC?

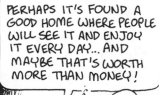

PERHAPS IT'S FOUND A GOOD HOME WHERE PEOPLE WILL SEE IT AND ENJOY IT EVERY DAY... AND MAYBE THAT'S WORTH MORE THAN MONEY!

YOU KNOW... YOU SOUND LIKE YOU'RE THINKING RIGHT TO ME, LUCY McKENZIE!

BATIUK & AYERS

The reason I am writing is to tell you how touched I've been at Lucy McKenzie's Alzheimer's and the very sensitive way in which you've presented it, along with a bit of very gentle humor.

You see, my husband is now in the Alzheimer's unit of a nursing home. He was diagnosed a couple of years ago, and finally last December admitted to long-term care when I couldn't manage at home anymore, even with good help. I go to see him every day, and it's still hard to believe this has happened to this vibrant, bright, creative, and very funny man. It's a long sad good-bye, but it has made me very aware of how many kind, caring friends and acquaintances are out there and what tremendous support is available.

Thank you, thank you, Tom, for doing what you are doing in your own unique and kind manner.

—*Jacky Woike*, Houston, Texas

You and Chuck Ayers receive my warmest commendation for raising social awareness, in a dignified and charmingly lighthearted way, relative to such traditionally taboo dimensions of the human condition as Alzheimer's. . . .

—*Dan Kane*, Gates Mills, Ohio

ARE YOU READY FOR CHOIR PRACTICE, LIL?

MAYBE YOU'D BETTER GO ON BY YOURSELF, LUCY!

I FEEL A MAJOR BOUT OF THE FLU COMING ON!

DO YOU WANT ME TO CALL A DOCTOR?

NO... I KNOW THERE'S A LOT OF THIS GOING AROUND WITHOUT PAYING SOMEONE TO TELL ME THAT!

BATIUK & AYERS

ARE YOU SURE YOU DON'T WANT ME TO CALL THE DOCTOR, LIL'?

WHAT'S THE POINT? THERE'S NOTHING A DOCTOR CAN DO ABOUT THE FLU!

BATIUK & AYERS

I KNOW... I MEANT TO GET OUR MONEY BACK FOR THE FLU SHOT!

GOODNIGHT EVERYBODY!

GOODNIGHT, LUCY...TELL LILLY WE HOPE SHE FEELS BETTER!

BATIUK & AYERS

47

48

I DON'T UNDERSTAND IT... OUR STREET SHOULD BE RIGHT AROUND HERE SOMEWHERE....

BUT NONE OF THESE HOUSES SEEM TO LOOK FAMILIAR!

IT'S GETTING LATE AND LILLIAN IS GOING TO BE WORRIED ABOUT ME!

I'M WORRIED ABOUT ME!

HELLO...OH, LILLIAN...WE MISSED YOU AT CHOIR PRACTICE TONIGHT!

LUCY? NO...SHE LEFT SEVERAL HOURS AGO!

I WOULDN'T WORRY...SHE'S PROBABLY JUST OUT VISITING WITH SOME FRIENDS!

I TRIED TO FOLLOW THE DIRECTIONS THAT THEY GAVE ME AT THAT GAS STATION...BUT I STILL CAN'T SEEM TO FIND OUR STREET!

LILLIAN'S GOING TO BE SO WORRIED...I SHOULD'VE BEEN HOME OVER....

THREE HOURS AGO!

I WONDER WHERE LUCY COULD BE ALL THIS TIME?

I HOPE SHE WASN'T IN AN ACCIDENT!

I do not know your age group, but apparently you have been closely associated and observed the senior group, and also the middle-aged and the younger set.

Your cartoons indicate you have a heart especially for the seniors and their feelings; their appreciation for their loved ones who instilled ideals, their memories of youthful years, and their current fears and sadness of approaching Alzheimer's disease.

Those two pictures in the paper . . . say volumes.

We all know an Ed Crankshaft, his faults and humanness. *Crankshaft* has become my favorite comic strip. Your cartoon strip tends to promote teaching and understanding, as well as humor. Best wishes for a long, fruitful career.

—*Lula Mae Winegar*, Knoxville, Tennessee

I am an older lady—who *never* writes about a comic strip—but you have struck a feeling to me and my friends who have seen other friends with such a disabling disease, who were independent and useful, laid low by age or what have you. It scares the devil out of us. So we thank you for showing such feeling and understanding for all of us. . . .

—*Shirley S.*, North Tonawanda, New York

Not long ago, your strip, *Crankshaft*, featured Alzheimer's disease and its effects on family and friends. As you came to realize, this is a difficult subject to address. Through your work though, you were able to convey to the public there is a lighter side.

The Indiana Health Care Association would like to commend you for your efforts in this arena. . . .

. . . thank you, and congratulations on a job well done.

—*Richard L. Butler*, former executive vice president,
Indiana Health Care Association, Indianapolis, Indiana

PHYSICALLY YOU SEEM TO BE FINE, LUCY...BUT, JUST TO BE ON THE SAFE SIDE, I'D LIKE TO HAVE YOU CONSULT A NEUROLOGIST!

BUT, IF I'M OK... WHY DO I NEED ANOTHER DOCTOR?

WHY CAN'T I JUST QUIT WHILE I'M AHEAD?

WE'LL MAKE AN APPOINTMENT FOR YOU WITH THE NEUROLOGIST AND WE'LL LET YOU KNOW WHEN IT IS!

THANK YOU!

ARE YOU SURE THIS IS A GOOD IDEA, LIL'? AFTER ALL... THE DOCTOR DID SAY THAT I SHOULD AVOID FAST FOODS!

THIS ISN'T THAT FAST!

BATIUK & AYERS

*T*he recent series of *Crankshaft* on Alzheimer's disease has really touched my heart. It touches on the very real problems encountered in caring for these patients. I am a nursing faculty member and Alzheimer's disease is an area that I teach. May I use your cartoons as I address this difficult situation in my classroom for student nurses?

I have enjoyed the *Crankshaft* series since the *Journal Star* started carrying it and generally save each strip, especially those that deal with health-related issues. You have really managed to hit the nail on the head in many situations. Keep it up!

—*Bonnie L. Allen, RN, M.S.,* Methodist Medical Center of Illinois, Peoria, Illinois

57

WHENEVER I NEEDED CHEERING UP, MY MOTHER AND I WOULD COME UP HERE TO OUR SECRET PLACE WHERE SHE'D TELL ME STORIES OR WE'D JUST SIT AND TALK!

DID IT WORK?

YOU BET!

IN FACT, ONE JANUARY WE CAME UP HERE AND FOUND SOME CHRISTMAS PRESENTS UNDER THE BED THAT MY MOTHER FORGOT TO GIVE US!

TELL ME A STORY, LUCY... A CHRISTMAS STORY!

WELL, IF WE'RE GOING TO TELL A CHRISTMAS STORY... WE'D BETTER DO IT RIGHT!

ONE CHRISTMAS...WHEN I WAS A LITTLE GIRL ABOUT YOUR AGE...

WHEN I WAS A LITTLE GIRL ABOUT YOUR AGE, MY FAVORITE PART OF THE YEAR WAS THE ANNUAL CHRISTMAS RECITAL AT THE HOME OF MY PIANO TEACHER, MRS. VANNESKI!

'I'D PRACTICE EVEN HARDER AS THE DAY FOR THE RECITAL GREW CLOSER!'

LUCY... STOP PRACTICING AND COME TO BED ALREADY!!

58

CRANKSHAFT

BY BATIUK & AYERS

OUR CHRISTMAS PIANO RECITAL WAS ALWAYS MY FAVORITE PART OF THE YEAR....

AND ONE YEAR IN PARTICULAR WILL ALWAYS STAND OUT IN MY MEMORY!

EACH YEAR AT THE END OF THE CHRISTMAS RECITAL WE'D ALL GATHER AROUND THE PIANO TO SING CAROLS!

MY PIANO TEACHER, MRS. VANNESKI, WOULD CHOOSE HER BEST STUDENT TO ACCOMPANY US AT THE PIANO!

AND CAN YOU GUESS WHO SHE HAD CHOSEN TO PLAY THE ACCOMPANIMENT AT THE RECITAL THAT YEAR?

NO....

BATIUK & AYERS

ME!

HEE! HEE! I KNEW THAT!

59

AND SO MY PIANO TEACHER, MRS. VANNESKI, HAD CHOSEN ME TO ACCOMPANY THE CAROLERS AT THE END OF OUR CHRISTMAS RECITAL!

'WHEN THE DAY OF THE RECITAL ARRIVED IT WAS FROSTY AND COLD OUTSIDE...'

'INSIDE, HOWEVER, I WAS QUITE WARM!'

YOU'RE NOT GOING ANYWHERE WITH THIS TEMPERATURE, LUCY MCKENZIE!

SO INSTEAD OF PLAYING ACCOMPANIMENT FOR THE CAROLERS AT THE CHRISTMAS RECITAL, I WAS HOME SICK WITH THE FLU!

I HAD LOOKED FORWARD TO IT SO MUCH THAT AS I LAY THERE IN BED I COULD ALMOST HEAR THEM SINGING!

GOD REST YE MERRY GENTLEMEN...

LET NOTHING YOU DISMAY...

AFTER A FEW MOMENTS, I REALIZED THAT THE CHRISTMAS MUSIC I WAS HEARING WASN'T IN MY IMAGINATION!

TO SAVE US ALL FROM SATAN'S FIRE...WHEN WE HAD GONE ASTRAY...

OHH, TIDINGS OF COMFORT AND JOY!

BATIUK & AYERS

♪♫ IT CAME UPON A MIDNIGHT CLEAR....

THAT GLORIOUS SONG OF OLD...

SO EVEN THOUGH I HAD THE FLU, I DIDN'T MISS PLAYING FOR THE CHRISTMAS RECITAL!

AFTER THE CAROLS WERE SUNG, MOTHER INVITED EVERYONE INSIDE FOR A CUP OF HOT COCOA... IT WAS A CHRISTMAS NONE OF US WOULD EVER FORGET....

ESPECIALLY THOSE WHO CAME DOWN WITH THE FLU THE NEXT DAY!

THERE YOU ARE, YOUNG LADY...WHERE HAVE YOU BEEN ALL THIS TIME?

IT'S A SECRET!

61

WE'RE BUYING THIS CD FOR OUR NEIGHBOR'S BOY WHO IS FOURTEEN!

DO YOU THINK HE'LL LIKE IT? ACTUALLY, HE'LL LOVE IT!

BEFORE YOU BUY THIS CD FOR YOUR NEIGHBOR'S SON....

DO YOU REALIZE THAT IT CONTAINS SOME EXPLICIT LYRICS?

YES...THAT'S WHY WE'RE GETTING IT!

EXACTLY... MOST OF THE TIME YOU CAN'T UNDERSTAND THE LYRICS AT ALL!

63

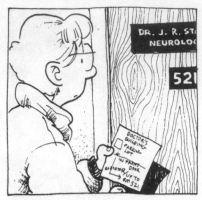

You have taught me the meaning of *poetry* . . . "A poet is a creative artist of great imagination and expressive gifts and special sensitivity in his medium." You *do* understand people. I hope you understand yourselves as well. The Lucy episode is heartbreaking. It is too accurate to believe you have brought this to us from anything other than personal experience. . . . all seniors' worst nightmare.

Thank you for your gift.

—A *Crankshaft* devotee, San Marino, California

*T*hank you for the beautiful, wordless essays on Alzheimer's—you must have been inspired to do this. Sometimes, the funnies aren't funny at all, are they? By providing these glimpses of the great sorrow associated with this dreadful disease, your pictures convey more than words—far more.

—*Lorna Schofield*, Mt. Lake Terrace, Washington

I have been following with great interest your series on Lucy's problems with Alzheimer's disease in *Crankshaft*. I was sure I knew what was wrong before the diagnosis, having observed the progression of this devastating illness in my husband's father.

So many things happen that are heartbreaking: confusion; wild imagination and fear; total inability to maintain personal finances and a checkbook; losing his driver's license; depression; anger. There are also funny things—like the black-and-white checked pants with the yellow plaid shirt and a blue necktie; and the uninhibited comments on everything from kids to neighbors to the preacher's sermon! (Once my father-in-law leaned out the passenger window and shouted an insult to another driver—much to my husband's dismay since the guy was twice his size and half his age!) There are the moments, too, of pathos (which you have done *very* well), like the time Dad talked about building his house and how proud he was of his work. He did build it all, but now has forgotten how to zip up his jacket.

As you can tell, you really touched my heart with your column. The quotation from the Book of Job really got to me. I look forward to reading *Crankshaft*, and I had to tell you what a fine job you are doing. You have the striking ability to provide a mirror that shows us the way we are in all our frail humanity. . . . It helps to know we are not alone.

—*Shirley Morris*, Hartford City, Indiana

 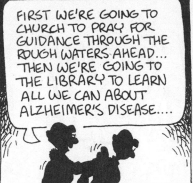 

*T*he story developed over time, just as the disease itself does, with forgetfulness moving into deeper periods of fear and finally into acknowledgment and diagnosis.

I think it's a wonderful and sensitive look at a horrible and frightening scourge. Not everyone agrees. The *Sun-Times* has received letters complaining that it's not a proper subject for the comics pages.

So has Batiuk, who writes the strip from Medina, Ohio. Ayers does the artwork. Most of the letters have been supportive, Batiuk said. But some have asked what a dreary subject like Alzheimer's is doing in the comics. "It's too painful," as one letter-writer to the *Sun-Times* put it.

Other readers were more appreciative. "I don't think you realize how much the last few *Crankshaft* comics have helped. I cut them out to remind myself how this awful thing affects" our family. . . .

. . . Strips like *Crankshaft* and the Alzheimer's episode have the opportunity to teach about hope, family values, and provide education, all without sugar-coated reality. . . .

I never want to face the struggle that Lucy is. But if it happens, I hope I have someone like Lil around to help me through it.

—Column by Tom Sheridan
Reprinted with permission, the *Chicago Sun-Times* © 1998

*I*must just drop a word this morning about *Crankshaft*. It's always excellent—I never know what to expect—but your interlude with the McKenzie sisters is a stroke of genius. For genius involves the heart as well as the head.

And the strip this morning, where Pam sees off Miss McKenzie and then goes down to embrace her father silently—and he grumps out "What now?"—is the best yet in understatement.

I've about given up on the "comics." most of them are sick or smart-alecky, fit only for sophomores. But I look forward to *Crankshaft* every morning—and this morning went over to my neighbor's house to share it with him.

—*Elmo Howell,* Memphis, Tennessee

I saw a strip yesterday called *Crankshaft*. . . .

It's about an old geezer who's living with his daughter and her husband, and it's well written, and also well drawn. Clear, in-depth, pictures. The storytelling is excellent. All of a sudden, apparently one of the two sisters who had been treated sort of casually and mostly in gag material started to develop symptoms—and he would come back to it now and then—and yesterday, this whole week, there has been a confirmation that the sister has Alzheimer's.

I thought his stuff was as touching as *anything* I ever read in the comics. I was never touched by Raven Sherman's burial in the way I was touched by this guy's handling of this Alzheimer's material. There was hardly any dialogue, it was mostly told in pictures. . . . It just broke my heart when I read it, I was so moved by it. . . .

. . . I was touched in the same way that when you look at a political cartoon, you can know and feel the whole power of the idea behind it. You realize that it's a single, primitive drawing that is trying to provoke something. And he did it. He evoked it successfully. . . .

. . . These last few days, I was so touched by the intelligence and sensitivity of the material. . . .

—Interview with Gil Kane, legendary comics artist in *The Comics Journal*, April 1996

CAN WE GO TO WOOLWORTH'S, MOMMY?

PLEASE!?

I JUST LOVE COMING IN HERE AND SMELLING THE WAFFLES AND POPCORN!

...AND ALL OF A SUDDEN I WAS REALLY IN THE MOOD FOR SOME POPCORN!

WHATEVER IS BOTHERING YOU, LIL' ...IT CAN'T BE ALL THAT BAD!

I GUESS THAT'S ONE THING ABOUT KNOWING THAT YOU HAVE SOMETHING LIKE ALZHEIMER'S...YOU SORT OF THINK 'WHAT COULD BE WORSE THAN THIS?'!

TRYING TO PAY FOR IT...!

WE'VE GOT OVER A THOUSAND DOLLARS IN MEDICAL BILLS THAT OUR INSURANCE WON'T COVER... AND I DON'T KNOW WHERE WE'RE GOING TO GET THE MONEY TO PAY THEM!

THAT'S NOT A PROBLEM... **I'VE** GOT THE MONEY!

YOU'VE GOT A **THOUSAND DOLLARS**!?

THAT'S RIGHT...AND PROBABLY A **WHOLE** LOT MORE!

YEARS AGO FATHER OPENED A SMALL SAVINGS ACCOUNT FOR ME AT HIS BANK....

IT WAS SUPPOSED TO BE A DOWRY BUT, AFTER A WHILE, I JUST KEPT IT AS A RAINY DAY ACCOUNT....

AND IF HAVING ALZHEIMER'S DOESN'T QUALIFY AS A RAINY DAY, THEN I DON'T KNOW WHAT DOES!

REMEMBER ALL THOSE STORIES YOU'D HEAR ABOUT LITTLE OLD LADIES WHO FORGOT ABOUT SAVINGS ACCOUNTS THEY HAD....

AND HOW YEARS LATER THEY'D HAVE THOUSANDS OF DOLLARS !?

WELL, WE'RE LITTLE OLD LADIES... SO LET'S GO SEE WHAT YOU'VE GOT!

SO YOU DON'T HAVE ANY CLUE AS TO HOW MUCH MONEY YOU HAVE IN THAT OLD SAVINGS ACCOUNT, LUCY?

NO... I'VE NEVER CHECKED IT!

I WANTED TO BE SURPRISED!

HMM... IT LOOKS LIKE WITH TIME AND COMPOUNDING INTEREST...YOU WERE ABLE TO ACCUMULATE QUITE A TIDY LITTLE SUM IN THIS ACCOUNT!

SEE, LIL'...I TOLD YOU WE WERE IN FOR A SURPRISE!

HOWEVER, IN THE EARLY EIGHTIES, WHEN WE HERE AT SILAS MARNER SAVINGS MERGED WITH A LARGER BANK... A NEW FEE STRUCTURE WAS INTRODUCED...

UNDER THE NEW FEE STRUCTURE, SINCE YOU NEVER USED THIS OLD ACCOUNT... YOU WERE CHARGED A TWENTY-DOLLAR-A-MONTH INACTIVE ACCOUNT FEE!

AND YOU KEPT CHARGING ME TWENTY DOLLARS **EVERY MONTH**!?

NO...WHEN YOUR ACCOUNT DROPPED BELOW A THOUSAND DOLLARS....

WE ADDED AN ADDITIONAL TEN-DOLLAR-A-MONTH FEE SINCE YOU NO LONGER MET OUR MINIMUM BALANCE REQUIREMENTS!

SO AFTER YOU FINISHED DEDUCTING ALL OF YOUR FEES, HOW MUCH MONEY WAS LEFT IN OUR ACCOUNT?

ACTUALLY, SINCE YOU NEVER CLOSED THE ACCOUNT, WE CONTINUED TO DEDUCT MAINTENANCE FEES EVEN AFTER THE PRINCIPAL WAS DEPLETED....

SO ACTUALLY YOU OWE US....

WE OWE **YOU** MONEY FOR OUR **SAVINGS ACCOUNT**!?

YES...BUT GIVEN THE LONGEVITY OF THIS PARTICULAR ACCOUNT AND THE UNUSUAL CIRCUMSTANCES....

WE'RE WILLING TO WAIVE THE INTEREST PENALTY CHARGES ON THE MONEY YOU OWE US!

MAN, WHAT A DAY... I'M BEAT!

ALL I WANT TO DO FOR THE REST OF THE DAY IS JUST SIT BACK AND RELAX!

DAD, WE NEED YOUR HELP! LUCY McKENZIE HAS WANDERED OFF!

LUCY MUST HAVE BEEN HAVING PROBLEMS WITH HER MEMORY AGAIN BECAUSE SHE LEFT A NOTE SAYING SHE WAS GOING TO SCHMIDT'S MARKET TO GET SOME CRANBERRIES FOR OUR MOTHER!

SCHMIDT'S MARKET!? THAT'S BEEN GONE FOR YEARS! IN FACT, THAT'S WHERE THEY JUST BUILT THAT NEW....

CRANBERRIES?

QUICK GAS CONVENIENCE STORE

SELF SERV

BUY LOTTERY

LUCY!

LUCY!

MISS McKENZIE!

LUCY!

LUCY!

I wish to thank you and Chuck Ayers for the understanding and warm humor expressed in *Crankshaft* on the subject of Alzheimer's disease.

We . . . had a crusade for quite a few years to make the public see just that which you are addressing: glimpses of the past, rather than believing there is nothing left of the person who once was. . . .

. . . one cannot forget that there are four million victims out there and research will not help them now. All we can do is improve the quality of their care and educate the public to the magnitude of the problem.

—*Selly C. Jenny,* Alzheimer's Association, Orange, California

THAT ORCHESTRA CONCERT WAS SIMPLY HEAVENLY!

MEANWHILE, BACK ON PLANET EARTH...

WHAT ABOUT MEDICAID LIL... WON'T THAT PAY FOR SOME OF MY MEDICAL BILLS?

NOT REALLY... IN ORDER FOR MEDICAID TO HELP US, WE PRACTICALLY HAVE TO BE DESTITUTE!

ALTHOUGH AT THE RATE THESE MEDICAL BILLS ARE PILING UP....

SOMEHOW THESE BILLS WILL GET PAID, LIL... WE JUST HAVE TO HAVE FAITH!

I DO HAVE FAITH, LUCY....

UNFORTUNATELY...THESE PEOPLE WANT MONEY!

I HAVE TO DO AN INTERVIEW WITH AN OLDER PERSON AND I THOUGHT I'D INTERVIEW LUCY!

I DON'T SEE WHY NOT... BUT SHE'S HAVING SOME PROBLEMS WITH HER MEMORY THESE DAYS!

I AM **NOT**!!

I THINK SHE FORGETS THAT SHE CAN'T REMEMBER THINGS!

THANKS FOR HELPING ME WITH MY INTERVIEW FOR SCHOOL, LUCY!

I'M HAPPY TO HELP, MINDY!

OK, FIRST QUESTION... WAS THERE ANY BIRTHDAY IN PARTICULAR THAT MADE YOU FEEL OLDER?

I THINK IT WAS WHEN I HIT THE DREADED THIRTY....

THE SECOND TIME!

OK... MY NEXT QUESTION FOR MY SCHOOL INTERVIEW IS....

WHAT IS IT LIKE BEING OLDER?

IT'S LIKE SITTING AROUND ALWAYS WAITING FOR THE NEXT SHOE TO DROP!

87

I STILL HAVE A FEW MORE QUESTIONS FOR MY INTERVIEW FOR SCHOOL, LUCY!

GO AHEAD... I'M HAVING FUN!

OK, WHEN YOU GET OLDER... WHY DO THEY CALL IT YOUR GOLDEN YEARS?

BECAUSE IT STARTS TO GET VERY EXPENSIVE!

JUST A FEW MORE QUESTIONS, LUCY!

FINE!

DO YOU EVER THINK ABOUT DYING?

NO....

I WANT TO BE SURPRISED!

DO YOU FEEL A SENSE OF ACCOMPLISHMENT IN HAVING LIVED AS LONG AS YOU HAVE?

NO, NOT REALLY....

THE REAL FUN IS IN PAINTING THE PAINTING....

NOT SEEING IT HUNG ON THE WALL!

CRANKSHAFT BY BATIUK & AYERS

ONE LAST QUESTION FOR MY SCHOOL REPORT, LUCY....

DO YOU THINK OF YOURSELF AS A SENIOR CITIZEN?

OH, MY GOODNESS NO!

NO MATTER HOW OLD YOU GET....

YOU ALWAYS THINK OF THOSE PEOPLE OLDER THAN YOU AS SENIOR CITIZENS!

ONE DAY, OF COURSE, I'LL EVENTUALLY DIE....

AND THEN I'LL BE A SENIOR CITIZEN!

I've been a follower of your *Crankshaft* strip for quite some time, but only lately has it had special meaning for me.

I'm amazed at how you two are handling the Alzheimer's portion of your strip. My father died of this disease a few years ago and I'm sure he would have really liked your handling of this subject. I was really touched [at] how our little old lady was hiding in the attic with her doll. I think my father might have done the same thing—but the disease hit him so quickly he just forgot everybody and everything.

Many times he took off in the middle of the night only to be gone two or three days. The police were incredible the way they handled the situation when they found him. They called us and asked if we wanted them to pick him up, or just wait so we could come get him so he would not be frightened. They were very enlightened.

When I picked him up, they were parked just down the street so he would not be frightened by them. Police cars and officers can be very intimidating even to these sick people.

Many times he lost his car and claimed it stolen only to be found weeks later where he parked it and then walked ten miles home. God really protected him—he could have been robbed and beaten up—but this never happened.

I don't know why I'm telling you this except I had a feeling you were telling your story, not just a comic strip story. Your sensitivity and message comes across to me on this delicate subject. My father died a few years ago—but he was in a special place that some caring person told us to take him [to]. He was clean, happy, confused—but loved and well taken care of by these special people. He died not afraid and not alone. I hate this disease—I'm angry for what it did to him and many others. Thank God for sensitive people and thank you for your story and your special handling of this sickness. Sad times are handled a little easier when humor is present.

—*John Kaufman*, North Hollywood, California

91

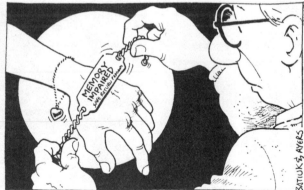

*T*hose of us who work at the San Diego Chapter of the Alzheimer's Association—both as staff and as volunteers—want you to know how much we appreciate your sensitive and caring approach to Alzheimer's victims.

We have a successful Safe Return program in San Diego county, and especially liked the recent series on wandering. Surely, many people will sign up with Safe Return as a result of your comic strip. Thanks from all of us.

—*Ronald C. Hendrix, Ph.D.,*
Alzheimer's Association, San Diego, California

I work at the La Fetra Center for Seniors, the senior center serving the city of Glendora, California. Recently, our staff has enjoyed (and appreciated the finesse with which you drew) your recent series of cartoon strips dealing with Alzheimer's disease and the much-needed Safe Return registration program.

Since last October, our city has been designated a California Healthy City by the State of California. Our Healthy Cities project is an Alzheimer's Awareness program, where we have sought to increase awareness in the city of the available resources for helping Alzheimer's patients, their families, and caregivers. The major components of the program were providing information, assistance, and follow-up to those seeking resources; educating professionals such as police and firemen, transportation personnel and ministers; sponsoring a support group for Alzheimer's caregivers; and increasing Safe Return registrations. After almost one year, we are happy to report that our project is succeeding and we will continue to provide this type of assistance to those in need. However, your innovative way of reaching individuals about this important issue so poignantly was something we wanted to applaud! . . .

—*Denise Mueller and Beth Busseau,* City of Glendora, California

ACTUALLY MY MEMORIES ARE STILL ALL THERE....

LOCKED INSIDE THESE TINY LITTLE GRAY CELLS!

I JUST CAN'T FIND SOME OF THE KEYS ANYMORE!

BYE... I'LL SEE YOU TOMORROW!

DON'T FORGET!

I WON'T... AND DON'T YOU FORGET EITHER!

WELL... I'M NOT MAKING ANY PROMISES!

SO HOW'S LUCY McKENZIE DOING?

SHE SEEMS TO BE GETTING MORE AND MORE FORGETFUL!

EH... THAT'S WHAT ALZHEIMER'S WILL DO TO YA!

HER MIND IS ALWAYS SWITCHING TRACKS IN THE MIDDLE OF THE STREAM!

BATIUK & AYERS

101

IT SURE GETS AWFULLY QUIET AROUND HERE THESE DAYS!

I KNOW....

I MISS THE PITTER-PATTER OF LITTLE FEET AROUND THE HOUSE...MAYBE WE SHOULD CONSIDER ADOPTING!

OH, LIL... I THINK WE'RE A LITTLE OLD FOR THAT!

I MEANT A CAT!

ANIMAL SHELTER

WE SHOULD BE ABLE TO ADOPT A NICE CAT HERE!

ARE YOU HERE TO DROP AN ANIMAL OFF?

NO...THIS IS A TAKE-OUT!

103

@#☆* CAT!! NOW I'LL PROBABLY HAVE TO GET A TETANUS SHOT!

I DON'T THINK SO, DAD... IT'S ONLY A SCRATCH!

IF I DON'T GET A SHOT I COULD GET LOCKJAW!!

I'D BE WILLING TO CHANCE IT!

ALL THOSE MCKENZIE SISTERS DO IS COMPLAIN ABOUT HOW THOSE KITTENS GET UNDER FOOT, RUIN THINGS, WON'T EAT THIS OR THAT, OR WON'T USE THEIR LITTER BOX...

YEAH...THEY'RE HAVING A BALL WITH THEM!

I'M SURE THOSE NEW KITTENS WILL BE ADAPTING TO LIFE AT THE MCKENZIE HOUSE PRETTY QUICKLY!

Afterword

This book is very special. Between its covers you will find courage, hope, and humor in perhaps an unlikely place—people with Alzheimer's disease and their caregivers.

Providing care for a loved one with Alzheimer's disease is one of the most heartbreaking, frustrating, and thankless jobs in the world. All of a sudden, the person who taught you to look both ways before crossing the street now wanders out of your home and gets lost. The person who promised to love, honor, and cherish you may not even remember your name. Medical and long-term care bills threaten to bankrupt you and your loved ones.

While humor may be in very short supply in these circumstances, the thousands of family caregivers the Alzheimer's Association works with each year tell us that a good sense of humor is one way they keep themselves "sane" and healthy.

With their gentle humor, Tom Batiuk and Chuck Ayers have compassionately taken on one of the most devastating diseases our society has known and enlightened us all. Through their touching, funny, and brave comic strip characters like Lucy and Lillian McKenzie, Ralph and Helen, Mindy, and that lovable curmudgeon Ed Crankshaft, we have seen how Alzheimer's disease can affect not only persons with the disease and their caregivers, but an entire community.

The Alzheimer's Association and its national network of more than 200 chapters are grateful that Tom and Chuck chose to educate their readers about wandering, a potentially life-threatening behavior associated with Alzheimer's disease. Raising awareness about this issue is critical, given that more than 60 percent of people with this disease will wander at least once at some point in the disease process.

Today, there are four million people in the United States with Alzheimer's disease. If you are a caregiver, you are not alone. Please contact the Alzheimer's Association at (800) 272-3900 to learn about Alzheimer's disease, support groups, research, respite care, and registering a loved one in the Alzheimer's Association's Safe Return Program.

Safe Return is the only nationwide program that assists in the identification and safe, timely return of people with Alzheimer's disease or other dementia who wander and become lost.

May this book bring some joy and comfort to those who read it. As family caregivers and caring professionals know, a smile can make all the difference.

—Edward Truschke
President and CEO, Alzheimer's Association